Young Explorers

Around Berlin

Text by Daniela Celli

Illustrations by Laura Re

whitestar kids

FOR PARENTS

Visiting a metropolis like Berlin with children can seem complicated and exhausting, but I assure you that it is also an incredibly fun and special experience. Every inch of this city is full of history, like the unusual traffic light men, or the touching stories of attempts to cross the Berlin Wall, or funny traditions like swimming in the lake dressed as Santa Claus. There are also educational opportunities, where the mistakes of the past can teach us to raise a better generation for the future.

THIS GUIDE IS YOUR GOLDEN TICKET TO AN ADVENTURE THAT WILL FILL YOUR FAMILY WITH WONDER.

These pages contain four itineraries, written and designed for your children. You will be guided by Berlin's most beloved animal to the most entertaining museums and the most fascinating monuments, squares, fountains, and parks.

This book is the perfect way to get your trip started, or even for a pretend vacation at home. I will describe everything that my children loved and that will, I hope, also enchant you and your little explorers.

Daniela Celli

To Simona, and the walnut shells that started it all.

GUTEN MORGEN, KINDER. NICE TO MEET YOU!

My name is Herr Bär Alex and, as you have probably guessed, I am a bear. I will accompany you around Berlin, and I'm sure we'll have a great time together! We'll see Hansel and Gretel, visit the Frog Prince, turn into secret agents as we detect hidden "bugs," make one journey into the past and one into the future, and then search for animals and ... traffic light men!

We'll do all this and much more. But how? Well, I have prepared for you FOUR DIFFERENT ITINERARIES that will guide us as we discover the most fantastic sites around the city, both inside and outside the historic center. Each route starts with A MAP where you can see the planned stops along with some useful and interesting facts. I have also organized games to play for some extra fun between one route and the next.

GUT, ARE YOU READY TO GO?

CONTENTS

ITINERARY 1

ITINERARY 2

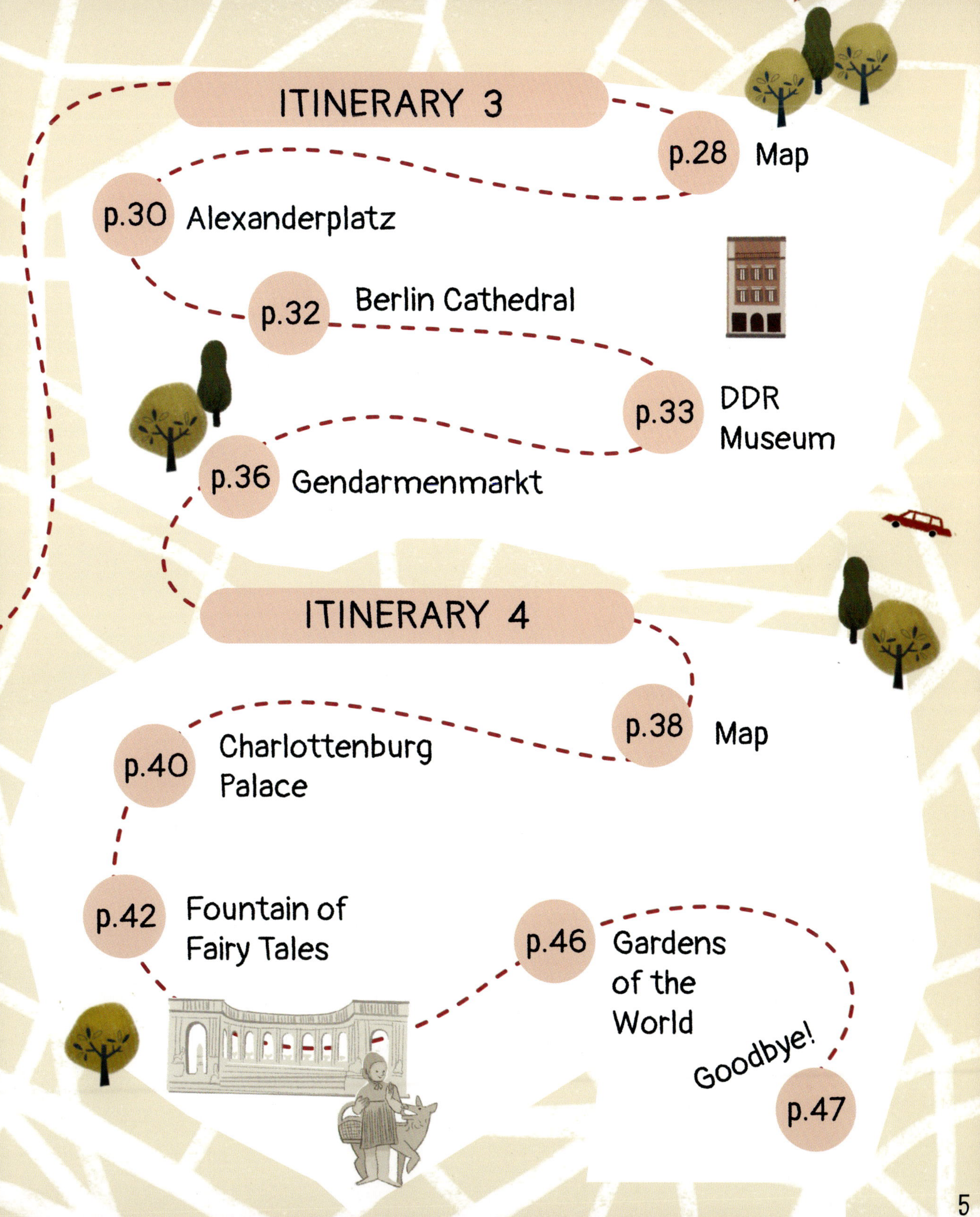

BERLIN

*Hallo Kinder,
willkommen in Berlin!*

ITINERARY 1

For our first day in Berlin, we will enter the city like kings through its ANCIENT GATE. We will learn lots of interesting details about chariots and horses, take a walk around the top of a building, and travel in a time machine for a journey into the future and another into the past. Then we will finally relax in a wonderful park, listening to the sweet notes of a giant carillon.

- **The Berlin Bear**

Until recently, the name *Berlin* was thought to be from the German word *Bär* meaning BEAR. However, it most likely derives from the Slavic word *berl*, for the SWAMP that once occupied this part of Germany.

WHATEVER THE TRUTH, THERE IS NO DOUBT THAT THE BEAR—HAHA THAT'S ME—IS THE MOST BELOVED ANIMAL IN BERLIN AND HAS BEEN THE SYMBOL OF THE CITY FOR CENTURIES.

- **The traffic light men**

As you walk through the streets of Berlin, you'll surely notice the UNUSUAL CHARACTERS populating traffic lights. The red one is vigilant and proud, and the green one is cheerful and energetic. These are the *Ampelmännchen*, created in 1961 to prevent accidents due to the increase in road traffic.

THEY'RE CERTAINLY HARD TO MISS!

BRANDENBURG GATE

Guten Morgen, children, and welcome
to the first stop on our journey!

The Brandenburg Gate is the most famous monument in Berlin. It was commissioned by the KING OF PRUSSIA in 1788 and was inspired by the arcades that decorated the ancient Greek city of ATHENS, which also led to the idea of placing the Greek goddess of VICTORY, *Nike*, at the helm of a great chariot drawn by four horses.

• The "horse thief"

In 1806, after defeating the Prussian army, NAPOLEON dismantled the quadriga (the chariot pulled by the four horses) and sent the pieces to Paris in 12 wooden crates. Fortunately, following the Battle of Waterloo less than a decade later, Nike and the horses were safely returned home.

DAS IST GUT!

• The sole survivor

During World War II the chariot was severely damaged by bombing and had to be restored several times. The only original piece left is the HEAD OF ONE HORSE, which can be found on display in the *Märkisches Museum.*

• The gateway ... to success

The *Brandenburger Tor* was one of the main entrances to Berlin, but citizens were only allowed to pass through the side openings. The main gate in the middle was reserved for the king and other powerful authorities.

OBVIOUSLY, THIS RULE NO LONGER APPLIES AND IT IS NOW OPEN TO EVERYONE. INDEED, IT IS SAID THAT WALKING THROUGH THE MIDDLE GATE WILL BRING YOU GOOD FORTUNE!

REICHSTAG

What is that spectacular glass dome that can be glimpsed behind the Brandenburg Gate?
Folgt mir, Kinder. Follow me, let's check it out!

The *Reichstag* is a large building where GERMAN POLITICIANS gather to make important decisions that affect the whole country. It is a fascinating place full of LEGENDS, such as the GHOST of an old parliamentarian who is said to wander the corridors on the darkest nights, or the story of an ancient lucky coin hidden somewhere among the stones.

WHAT DO YOU THINK? SHALL WE LOOK FOR IT?

• **Eco-friendly**
The DOME OF THE PARLIAMENT BUILDING hides a secret: the inner cone contains a complex heat recovery system that provides heating naturally for the whole building as well as illumination!

DON'T FORGET TO PICK UP THE AUDIO GUIDE FOR CHILDREN AT THE ENTRANCE!

• A walk into the sky

The dome, 75 feet (23 meters) high and 131 feet (40 meters) wide, is without doubt the most fascinating part of the building. It's made of glass and steel with a giant trunk-like CONE inside that is lined with 360 mirrors!

As you climb the spiral ramp that runs all the way to the top, not only can you enjoy a 360° view of Berlin, but on sunny days the mirror cone reflects the light, creating a magical atmosphere.

FUTURIUM

Hallo, Freunde, ready to travel into the future?

Along the banks of the *Spree* River, a stone's throw from the PARLIAMENT BUILDING, there is a fascinating free museum inhabited by robots, humanoids, and talking refrigerators.

• An authentic time machine

Spread over three large floors, the *Futurium* is an authentic TIME MACHINE made up of 800 glass panels, open to all those who wonder what our future might be like: How will we live? What kind of houses will we have? What will we eat?

IF YOU WANT TO KNOW THE ANSWERS, THIS IS THE PLACE FOR YOU!

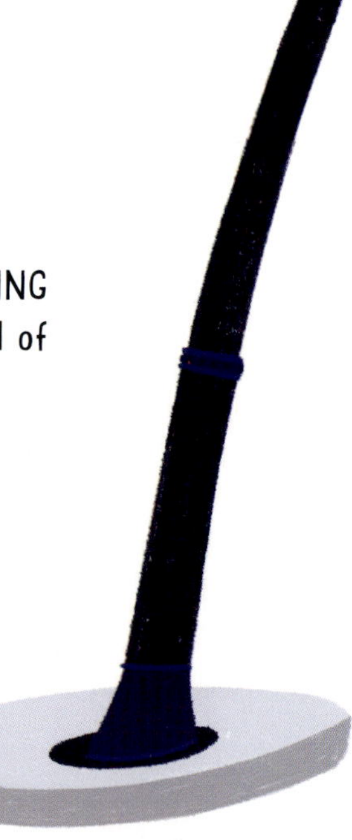

• An unusual work of art

The square in front of the Futurium contains an INTERESTING SCULPTURE created by a group of Berlin artists, composed of a huge rotating plate balanced on a pole.

MAKE SURE TO BE HERE AT NOON IF YOU WANT TO SEE IT IN ACTION!

NATURAL HISTORY MUSEUM

And now let's take a trip to the past!

The *Museum für Naturkunde* is a fantastic place to discover the development of life on our planet. Founded more than 200 years ago, it has collected thousands of ARTIFACTS from the greatest discoveries made by EXPLORERS around the world: prehistoric animals, dinosaur skeletons and eggs, giant meteorites, and primitive birds.

• The giraffe dinosaur

One of the museum's most famous attractions is the skeleton of a *Giraffatitan*, one of the largest sauropods in the world. This enormous animal, which lived about 150 million years ago, had a very long neck and giraffe-like body.

TIERGARTEN

How about some *Entspannung*?
That's how we say "relaxation" in German!

With an area equal to 350 soccer fields, *Großer Tiergarten* is Berlin's GREEN LUNG and the city's largest park. The Greater Animal Garden was once a HUNTING RESERVE for the prince, but today it is a magnificent PARK, home to many wild animals. Here you can run, play, picnic, and even rent a rowboat or paddleboat on the lake called the *Neuer See*.

• The Angel of Peace

In the heart of the park there is the famous *Siegessäule*, a column more than 217 feet (66 meters) tall and built in 1873 to commemorate wartime victories. On its top stands the GODDESS OF VICTORY, a large bronze statue that weighs as much as 60 bears.

NOW FOLLOW ME TO THE TOP.
CAN YOU MAKE IT UP ALL 265 STEPS?

DO YOU HEAR IT TOO? THAT BEAUTIFUL SOUND?
COME ON, LET'S TAKE A LOOK!

• Un sehr *groß* carillon

On the edge of the park is a strange black granite tower that is actually a GIGANTIC MUSICAL INSTRUMENT! At 138 feet (42 meters), it contains 68 bells that ring every day at 12:00 PM and 6:00 PM.

ON PUBLIC HOLIDAYS, YOU CAN ATTEND GENUINE *CARILLONNEUR* CONCERTS.

Discovery Quest Seek and Find

a stuffed bear

one mug of beer

a Trabant car

a Berlin scarf

Another day exploring Berlin!

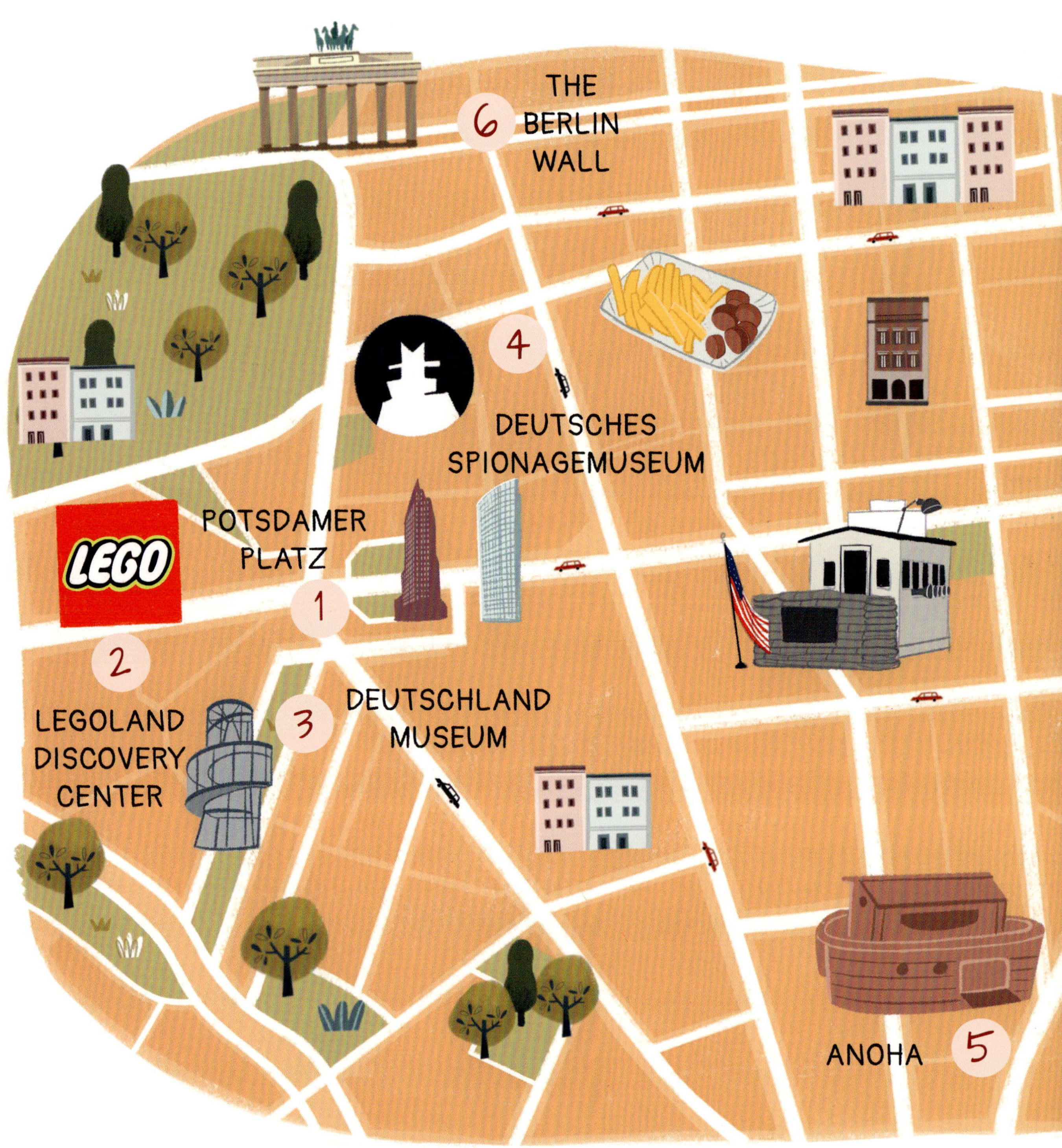

ITINERARY 2

Today our tour will start from a square full of interesting skyscrapers and streets. We will climb up to a viewing platform to admire the city from above and relax in the terrace café while we decide which museums to visit. Because, guess what? THERE ARE MORE MUSEUMS IN BERLIN THAN ANTS AT A PICNIC! Take a look at the map and pick which ones look the most interesting!

• **Walking works up an appetite**

Berlin is a *street food* paradise. Every neighborhood is brimming with markets, stalls, and food trucks full of delicacies. Popular FOODS include *Döner kebab*, a *pita* stuffed with meat, salad, onions, and spices; the legendary *currywurst*, a SLICED sausage covered in a spicy sauce; and *kartoffelpuffer*, a crispy POTATO PANCAKE.

I LOVE IT!

• **An excellent reward**

And of course, there is the *brezel*, also known as a *pretzel*, the star of every *Bäckerei* (bakery). This legendary ring-shaped "bread" with two knots owes its name to the word *pretiola*, meaning LITTLE REWARD. It was originally given as a prize to children who learned Bible verses by heart.

POTSDAMER PLATZ

We have now reached the most modern square in Berlin!

Completely rebuilt after the FALL OF THE WALL (see page 24), *Potsdamer Platz* was born from the ingenious minds of the best architects in the world, creators of unique skyscrapers, such as the *BlueMax Theater*, an immense GLASS THEATER with a 115-foot (35-meter) sphere inside, or the incredible *Sony Center*, a complex of seven buildings topped by a huge dome that symbolizes Japan's Mount Fuji and transforms into a colorful "umbrella" at night.

Name: Bahntower
Years of construction: 1998–2000
Height: 338 feet (103 meters)
Floors: 22
Special features: Curved façade covered in glass.

Name: Atrium Tower
Year of construction: 1997
Height: 348 feet (106 meters) (the tallest in the square)
Floors: 26
Special features: It has a huge emerald-green cube on top.

Name: Kollhoff Tower
Year of construction: 1999
Height: 331 feet (101 meters)
Floors: 25
Special features:
Shaped like a staircase with a viewing platform (Panorama Punkt) and café on top.

- **Watch out for traffic**

A hundred years ago *Potsdamer* was a crossroads of 100,000 people, 20,000 cars, hundreds of carriages, and at least 600 trams a day!

In an attempt to control this traffic jam, the nation's first traffic signal was installed in 1924, consisting of a CONTROL TOWER on which a policeman sat, controlling the lights for five different sides.

Oh Mann, WHAT A BIG MESS!

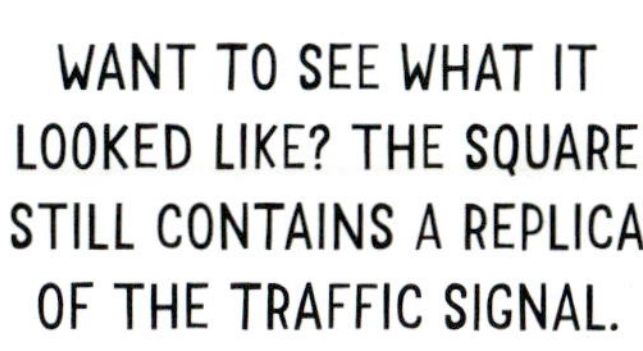

WANT TO SEE WHAT IT LOOKED LIKE? THE SQUARE STILL CONTAINS A REPLICA OF THE TRAFFIC SIGNAL.

LEGOLAND DISCOVERY CENTER

Do you love building things?

Inside *Miniland* you will be dropped into a Berlin made from more than TWO MILLION BRICKS! You will recognize the *Brandenburger Tor*, the *Reichstag*, and many other monuments. But that's not all. The factory reveals all the SECRETS of the production process, while the construction area allows you to unleash your creative side and build your own inventions. There's also the 4D cinema and other attractions, all made of LEGO® bricks!

• Play well

These legendary toys, now famous all over the world, were born in a small town in Denmark where OLE KIRK CHRISTIANSEN opened a wooden toy company in 1934. With the arrival of plastic, the carpenter had the idea of creating interlocking bricks, and voilá, an international success was born.

But why *LEGO®*?

THE WORD "LEGO" COMES FROM THE DANISH *LEG GODT*, WHICH MEANS "PLAY WELL."

DEUTSCHLAND MUSEUM

Are you the inquisitive type?

Yes? Then this is the place for you. At *Deutschland Museum* you can immerse yourself in a unique and engaging experience that travels through 2,000 years of GERMAN HISTORY. Discover the greatest events and INVENTIONS that have changed the world, the most treasured traditions, and even, *YUM*, TYPICAL GERMAN DISHES, through 4D animation, creative workshops, and extraordinary interactive INSTALLATIONS.

- **Smells of the past**

What makes this museum special is that it uses the latest technology to create incredibly realistic environments. Not only will you see and hear, you'll also touch and smell!

AN AUTHENTIC TIME MACHINE!

DEUTSCHES SPIONAGEMUSEUM

Are you fascinated by the world of spies?

In this museum, you will learn all about the secret world of espionage—from the stories of real agents who worked during the COLD WAR, to the stories of fictional characters, like the legendary JAMES BOND. Discover gadgets like camera pens or shoes with built-in phones, and transform yourself into a genuine 007 as you sweep for HIDDEN BUGS or try to navigate hallways armed with laser beams.

I'M TOO CLUMSY FOR THAT, BUT YOU GO AHEAD AND TRY TO GET THROUGH WITHOUT SETTING OFF *DER ALARM.*

• **Why are listening devices called "bugs"?**

These small devices, used to listen to people from a distance, are usually placed inside gaps in furniture or other hidden spots.

THE SAME PLACES WHERE REAL BUGS LIKE TO HIDE!

ANOHA,
THE CHILDREN'S WORLD OF THE JEWISH MUSEUM

Do you love animals?
(Roar! I certainly hope so!)

At Anoha you can hide inside the tentacles of an octopus, dance with a unicorn, and climb an anaconda.
No, *liebe Kinder*, I'm not making this up! Anoha's animals are extraordinary SCULPTURES made from RECYCLED MATERIALS that you can move, pet, feed, and even help climb a giant wooden Noah's Ark. ARE YOU STRONG ENOUGH TO LIFT UP YOUR BEAR FRIEND?

• Repairing the world

Tikkun Olam is a Jewish concept that means REPAIRING THE WORLD. Imagine the world is a big puzzle with pieces that sometimes get lost or broken. When we do good things, like helping others, being nice, or protecting nature, it's like we're putting the missing pieces back in place and making the world more beautiful. Anoha was created with this concept in mind.

ANOHA IS DESIGNED FOR CHILDREN AGES THREE TO TEN. ENTRANCE IS FREE, BUT REMEMBER TO BOOK YOUR VISIT IN ADVANCE!

THE BERLIN WALL

Let's take a trip back in time!

After WORLD WAR II Berlin was divided into two parts: West Berlin and East Berlin. Life was better in the West, and many people wanted to move there, so the eastern government built a giant concrete wall that was almost 13 feet (4 meters) high. No one was allowed to cross it without permission, and ARMED GUARDS patrolled it night and day to make sure no one tried to escape.

• Limited passage

Checkpoint Charlie was one of the few checkpoints where a limited number of people, such as journalists, military personnel, or ambassadors, could pass through the wall, but only with special permits that were strictly controlled by American and Soviet guards.

• But who was Charlie?

Charlie wasn't really a person. The name for checkpoint C comes from a special coded alphabet that matches letters with words to make them easier to understand by radio. WHAT WORD REPRESENTS THE FIRST LETTER OF YOUR NAME?

A - Alpha
B - Bravo
C - Charlie
D - Delta
E - Echo
F - Foxtrot
G - Golf
H - Hotel
I - India
J - Juliet
K - Kilo
L - Lima
M - Mike
N - November
O - Oscar
P - Papa
Q - Quebec
R - Romeo
S - Sierra
T - Tango
U - Uniform
V - Victor
W - Whiskey
X - X-Ray
Y - Yankee
Z - Zulu

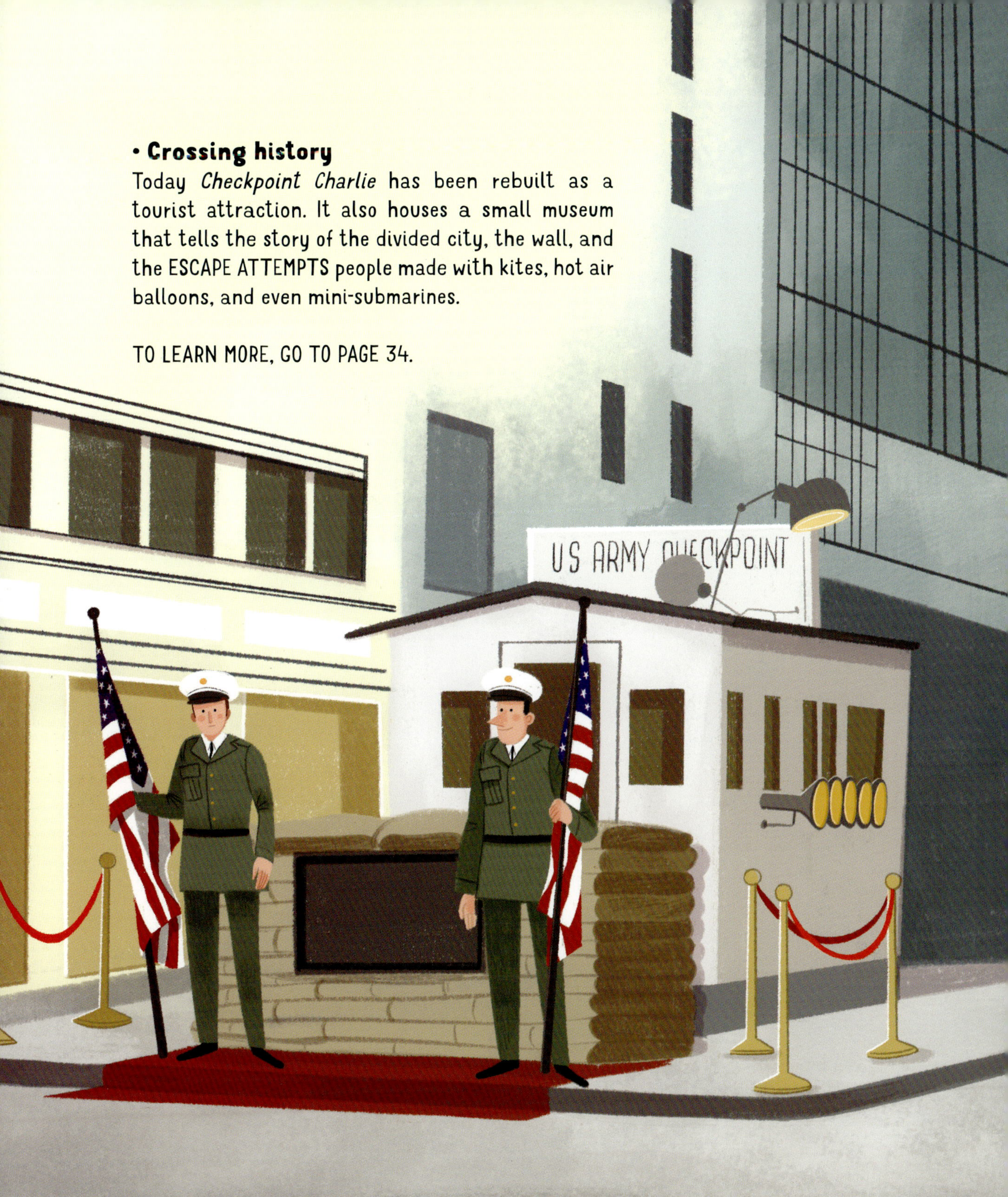

• Crossing history

Today *Checkpoint Charlie* has been rebuilt as a tourist attraction. It also houses a small museum that tells the story of the divided city, the wall, and the ESCAPE ATTEMPTS people made with kites, hot air balloons, and even mini-submarines.

TO LEARN MORE, GO TO PAGE 34.

LET'S LEARN SOME MORE ABOUT THE *BERLINER MAUER*

Wall statistics

Year of construction:
1961

Year it fell:
1989

Length of the wall dividing West and East Berlin:
27 miles (43 km)

Overall length:
96 miles (155 km)

Height:
13 feet
(4 meters)

Watchtowers:
302

Bunkers: 20

Sections guarded by dogs:
259

• Divided by a wall

Imagine that you can no longer see your friends or relatives because they live on the other side of a wall.

SADLY, THIS IS WHAT HAPPENED TO MANY FAMILIES IN BERLIN. SUDDENLY ONE DAY, THEY WERE NO LONGER ALLOWED TO HUG THEIR LOVED ONES.

• The fall

The wall stood for 28 long years. Then, on November 9, 1989, the government finally announced that EASTERN CITIZENS WERE FREE TO TRAVEL TO WEST GERMANY.

The checkpoints were opened and a crowd immediately gathered, armed with PICKS and HAMMERS to knock down the bricks that had kept them apart for so long.

IT WAS A WONDERFUL NIGHT OF CELEBRATION!

• What's left of the wall

The wall was torn down piece by piece, but fragments remain here and there to remind us of the importance of PEACE and FREEDOM. The *East Side gallery* is the largest remaining section. It stretches 0.8 miles (1.3 kilometers) and has been decorated by 118 artists from 21 countries, transforming it into an open-air art gallery.

The adventure continues!

ITINERARY 3

Today we will start our tour by climbing up a tower to eat ice cream while spinning through the Berlin sky.

We will listen to a concert by the largest organ in the country, board another time machine, and finish the day with the sweetest stop imaginable.

I'M READY, *UND DU?*

• **The Museum Island**

Stretching along the *Spree* River and connected to the mainland thanks to various convenient BRIDGES is an island populated by five museums surrounded by greenery. Some share the history of people who lived long ago, and others show beautiful paintings by famous artists, as well as statues and artifacts from the farthest corners of the world. It's a place full of history, stories, and adventures to imagine and experience.

• **More bridges than Venice!**

Berlin has 969 bridges crossing rivers, canals, and lakes. Some are very old, such as the *Jungfern* Bridge, while others have recently been rebuilt, like the much-loved *Oberbaumbrücke*, which has become a symbol of Berlin's rebirth. With its high towers and elegant arches, it feels like a fairy tale castle!

ALEXANDERPLATZ

Haha! Here we are in my favorite square,
the largest in Berlin!

Located in the heart of the city, *Alexanderplatz*, or *Alex*, as it is affectionately called by Berliners, stretches roughly as far as 12 soccer fields. Sadly, its name does not pay homage to your favorite bear guide, but to TSAR ALEXANDER I OF RUSSIA who visited Berlin in 1805. It was originally called *Ochsenplatz*, which in German means OXEN SQUARE.
This is where the cattle market was held.

ON ONE SIDE OF THE SQUARE, SET ABOVE A STONE MOSAIC REPRESENTING THE COMPASS ROSE, STANDS A HUGE AND RATHER UNIQUE CLOCK...

• Every time in the world
The *Urania Weltzeituhr* consists of a large cylinder with 24 sides, each of which corresponds to a different time zone. Inside the cylinder, there is a ring with colored numbers that rotate and indicate the time in major cities around the world.

• The TV tower

At 1,207 feet (368 meters), the *Fernsehturm* is the tallest building in Germany. It was built in 1969 to broadcast television signals but has now become an important tourist attraction. At about 666 feet (203 meters) there is a panoramic platform that can be reached with a *super elevator* that takes only 40 seconds to get to the top. Alternatively, you can climb up 986 steps.

I, UM, ATE TOO MANY PICKLES THIS MORNING.
WHAT DO YOU SAY WE TAKE THE ELEVATOR?

• Spin and Taste

At 679 feet (207 meters) there is a fantastic restaurant at the top of the tower that rotates 360 degrees twice every hour!

HOW ABOUT AN ICE CREAM? CHOCOLATE, VANILLA, OR STRAWBERRY?

BERLIN CATHEDRAL

We now stand before the *Berliner Dom*, the largest and most impressive church in Berlin.

It's so vast that even the GODDESS OF VICTORY COLUMN could fit inside without touching the top. The roof is formed by a giant BRIGHT GREEN DOME that you can bravely climb thanks to 270 steps! The view from the terrace is magnificent, and you can easily admire the beautiful tree-lined boulevard called *Unter den Linden*, the *Gendarmenmarkt*, and Museum Island.

• **Celestial music**

The interior of the cathedral is full of magnificent decorations, mosaics, and stained-glass windows, but the most surprising thing is a gigantic organ with 7,269 pipes, one of the largest in Germany.

I LOVE *DIE MUSIK*.
HOW ABOUT YOU?

DDR MUSEUM

Ready to step back in time and discover what life was like in East Germany?

After World War II, Germany was divided into two parts. East Germany was known as the DDR, or Deutsche Demokratische Republik (German Democratic Republic). Citizens lived with few freedoms, and the secret police controlled everything with the help of spies.

• A journey through time

At the DDR Museum, you can immerse yourself completely and interactively into everyday life under the shadow of the Berlin Wall. You can walk into a typical apartment, drive a *Trabant car*, sit at school desks, shop in a supermarket, wear period costumes, try out children's favorite toys, and discover the cartoons they were allowed to watch.

ABOUT 5,000 GERMANS, TIRED OF THIS TYRANNY, MANAGED TO ESCAPE OVER THE WALL, SOME IN RATHER SPECTACULAR FASHION. TURN THE PAGE TO LEARN MORE.

DARING ESCAPES

• An acrobatic undertaking

In 1962, the German acrobat *HORST KLEIN* decided to escape by exploiting his circus skills. He climbed onto the pylon of a disused electric cable and walked along the wire like it was a tightrope until he made it past the wall.

UNFORTUNATELY, HE WAS EVENTUALLY OVERCOME BY FATIGUE AND FELL, GETTING AWAY WITH TWO BROKEN ARMS AS THE PRICE FOR HIS FREEDOM.

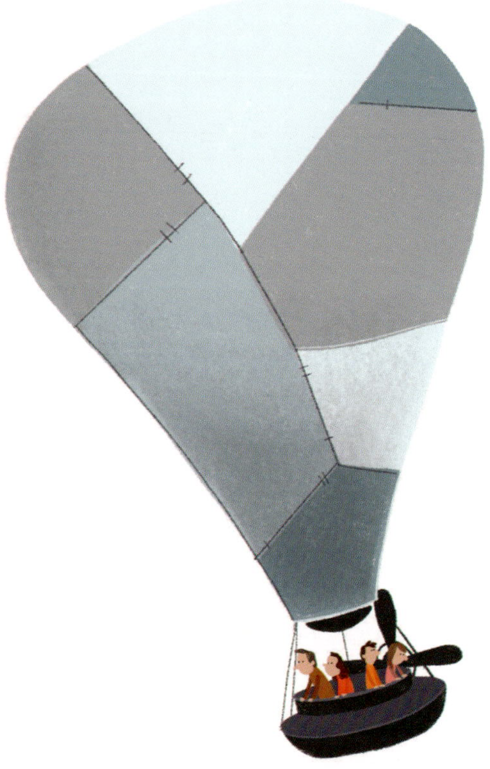

• Flying sheets

A mechanic and a bricklayer, with the help of their wives, built a rudimentary hot-air balloon using sheets and a fan motor!

AFTER TWO FAILED ATTEMPTS, THEY FINALLY MANAGED TO ESCAPE IN 1979, FLYING 1.6 MILES (2.5 KILOMETERS) UNTIL THE BALLOON CAME DOWN. BUT BY THEN THEY WERE ALREADY SAFE!

• Underground escape

In 1962, two Italian students devised a brilliant plan to help some friends and their relatives escape. Together with other volunteers, they spent months digging a long underground tunnel, stretching from the West to a cellar in the East.

TWENTY-NINE PEOPLE FOUND FREEDOM BEFORE THE TUNNEL BECAME FLOODED WITH WATER.

• Genuine escape artists

The three *BETHKE BROTHERS* were true escape artists. Ingo managed to escape across the river on a mattress. *HOLGER* connected a house in the East to a house in the West by shooting a cable across with a bow and arrow, then traveling across it thanks to a pulley system. *EGBERT* was then rescued by his brothers, who picked him up in a small camouflaged plane.

GENDARMENMARKT

Come children, another *schönen* square awaits us!

With its charming concert hall flanked by two beautiful twin domes, statues, and romantic streets illuminated with gas lighting, *Gendarmenmarkt* is considered the MOST BEAUTIFUL SQUARE IN BERLIN. Today, it is much beloved by citizens who come here for a walk or to enjoy a concert. However, this area was once used as barracks for the cuirassiers (mounted soldiers), which is why it is still called the MEN-AT-ARMS MARKET.

• Almost twins

It's impossible not to notice it right away. The French Cathedral and its German twin, both topped by an imposing domed tower, look almost exactly alike.

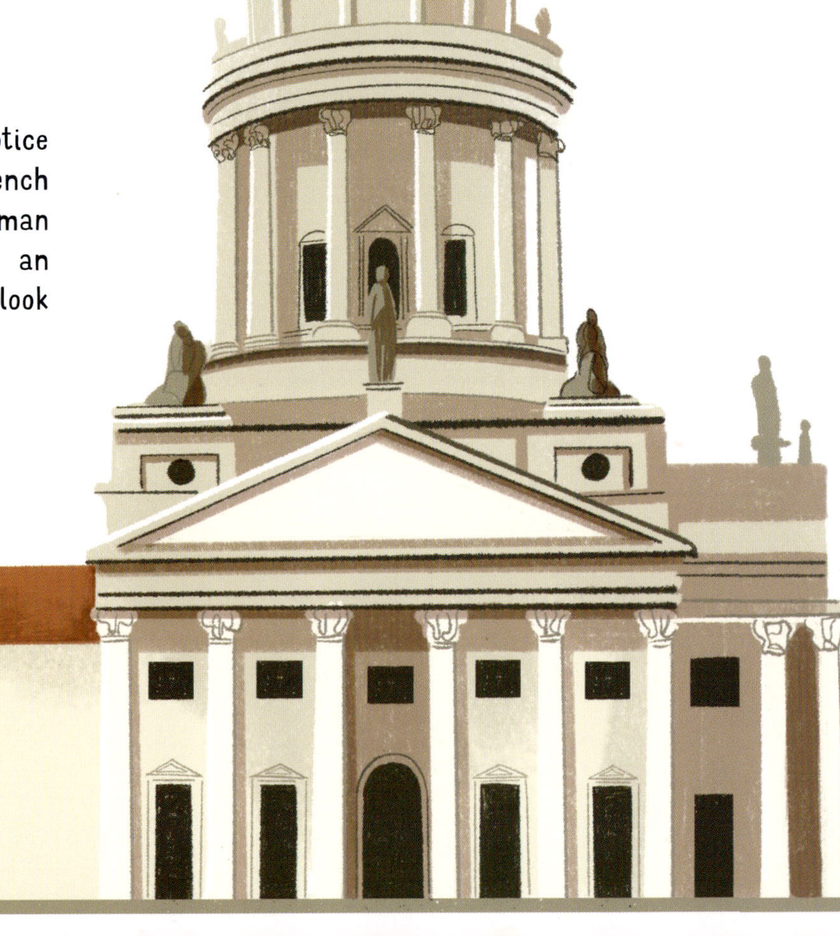

• Looking up

Pull out your binoculars because the top of the *Konzerthaus* has something interesting to see: Apollo, Greek god of the arts and music, drives a chariot pulled by strange animals that have the body of a lion with the head and wings of an eagle. They are called griffins, and in Greek mythology they were considered protectors and guardians.

TO BE HONEST, I FIND THEM A BIT SCARY. WHAT ABOUT YOU?

NOW WE HAVE REACHED THE SWEETEST STOP OF THE DAY. YUMMY!

• The Rausch chocolate shop

With 16,145 square feet (1,500 square meters) spread over three floors and a huge display of assorted chocolates, the *Rausch Schokoladenhaus* is one of the world's largest "chocolate houses." Founded in 1918, it is the kingdom of chocolate bars, cakes, ice cream, and truffles. The shop houses sculptures and monuments built from thousands of pounds of chocolate.

TRULY SUBLIME CREATIONS, WORTHY OF WILLY WONKA!

Let's go on our last adventure!

ITINERARY 4

Today we will travel from west to east to discover three fabulous green spots outside the city center. We will search for beavers and horned sheep in the gardens of a royal castle, board a boat, tell fairy tales in front of the splashing waters of frog princes, and finally travel all the way from Chile to China. NO, MY FRIENDS, I'M NOT KIDDING. JUST FOLLOW ME AND YOU'LL SEE!

- **Ready for takeoff!**
With more than 2,500 parks and gardens, the metropolis of Berlin is considered one of the *greenest* in Europe. Among the most unusual green spaces is the immense *Tempelhofer Feld,* which was originally the runway of an airport! However, there aren't any planes these days. Instead, you can ride roller skates, bicycles, skateboards, or a speedy *landsegler*, an unusual sailboat WITH WHEELS.

- **Unusual traditions**
With 3 rivers, 7 canals, and more than 50 lakes, many of which are swimmable, Berlin is considered a city of water. Among the most interesting traditions is that of the *Weihnachtsschwimmen*. Every year in December, a group of daredevils dressed as reindeer, Santa Claus, or other Christmas characters dive into the icy waters of the *Orankesee*. ARE THEY BRAVE OR JUST NUTTY?

CHARLOTTENBURG PALACE

We are now entering the summer residence of the queen of Prussia!

This marvelous castle, one of Berlin's largest and most sumptuous palaces, was commissioned by Queen SOPHIA CHARLOTTE more than 300 years ago. The queen loved art and music, so the elegant halls of the palace often hosted exhibitions and concerts by artists and musicians from all over the world. Unfortunately, the queen died very young. In homage to her, the king then ordered that the castle be named after her.

• ***Alle an Bord!***

The queen loved to take a boat back to her castle in Berlin. What do you say, shall we take one too? Numerous ferries along the Spree River link Charlottenburg with the city center.

READY TO HOP ABOARD!?

• A castle full of animals

The palace is surrounded by beautiful BAROQUE GARDENS where you can freely walk around the lakes and century-old trees, ride a bicycle, have a picnic, or play in the beautiful playground.

IN WINTER THERE IS EVEN A HILL FOR SLEDDING!

BUT YOU KNOW WHAT MY FAVORITE THING TO DO IS? Searching for all the animals hidden in the park: frogs, fish, birds, beavers, and even a flock of funny horned sheep!

CAN YOU FIND THEM ALL?

FOUNTAIN OF FAIRY TALES

We have arrived at one of Berlin's most popular fairy-tale settings!

The *Märchennbrunnen*, which means "fountain of fairy tales" in German, was inaugurated in 1914 to create an enchanted place for children to immerse themselves in the world of fairy tales. It is a truly magical place in an equally enchanting atmosphere: the *Volkspark Friedrichshain*, Berlin's oldest park!

• The fairy tales of the Brothers Grimm

The large fountain is composed of a central pool connected to nine smaller ones inside which there are seven mischievous frogs. One of these is, of course, the star of "The Frog Prince," from the extraordinary fairy tale made famous by the Brothers Grimm. BUT HE'S NOT ALONE!

All around the fountain, ten more statues represent nine of the stories so beloved by children: Hansel and Gretel, The Seven Ravens, Cinderella, Hans in Luck, Brother and Sister, Snow White and the Seven Dwarfs, Puss in Boots, Sleeping Beauty, and you will surely guess the name of the last fairy tale: a little girl next to a wolf with his tongue hanging out and a hungry look in his eyes...

IT'S LITTLE RED RIDING HOOD!

• Why are of Hansel and Gretel sitting on top of ducks?

According to one of the many versions of the fairy tale, after defeating the witch by pushing her into the oven, the two children travel back through the woods to return home, only to find themselves blocked by a river.

GUESS WHO HELPS THEM CROSS IT? THAT'S RIGHT, TWO DUCKS!

LET'S LEARN MORE ABOUT THE BROTHERS GRIMM

• Who were they?

Jacob and *Wilhelm Grimm* were born more than two centuries ago in *Hanau*, Germany. Although very different in character, the two brothers shared a great passion for literature and short stories. Fearing that many unwritten fairy tales would be lost over time, the brothers decided to collect them in a book they called CHILDREN'S AND HOUSEHOLD TALES.

• Fairy tale hunters

The Grimms lived together all their lives, even after Wilhelm married and had children. They spent their final years in Berlin in an apartment near the *Tiergarten* where they often went for walks. They were buried next to each other in the St. Matthäus Kirchhof Cemetery where, to this day, children and adults pay their respects by decorating the tombs with drawings depicting their famous fairy tales.

• Yikes! So scary!

To collect the fairy tales, the Grimms traveled from village to village in the German countryside, listening to tales told by grandmothers in front of the fire, or by anyone else with a story to share. Sometimes the stories were very scary!

AFTER COMPARING THE DIFFERENT VERSIONS THEY ENDED UP REWRITING MORE THAN 200 FAIRY TALES!

THE FAIRY TALES COLLECTED BY THE TWO BROTHERS OFTEN HAVE DARK AND GLOOMY SETTINGS OF FORESTS POPULATED BY WITCHES, OGRES, AND WOLVES. LATER, THE ORIGINAL VERSIONS WERE SOFTENED TO MAKE THEM LESS FRIGHTENING TO CHILDREN.

GARDENS OF THE WORLD

Ready for a trip around the world?

Nein, meine lieben Kinder, your dear bear has not gone completely insane. The *Gärten der Welt* is a gigantic BOTANICAL PARK that contains themed gardens inspired by the continents and habitats of the world, from Bali to Japan, China to Korea, as well as Italian and English gardens, and even a hedge maze of 1,225 evergreen yew trees that reach 7 feet (2 meters) high.

IF I STAND ON TIPTOE, MAYBE I CAN PEEK OVER THE TOP. DO YOU THINK YOU CAN MAKE IT ALL THE WAY TO THE TOWER IN THE CENTER WITHOUT GETTING LOST?

• Fun for everyone

In addition to the themed gardens, this formidable park offers access to TROPICAL GREENHOUSES, art pieces to discover, a treasure hunt, a walkway that rises 394 feet (120 meters) into the air, fun at the amazing playgrounds, and finally, a ride on a CABLE CAR that sways 115 feet (35 meters) above the park.

BE WARNED: SIX OF THE CABLE CARS HAVE A GLASS FLOOR! ARE YOU BRAVE ENOUGH TO GET IN?

I HOPE THAT BERLIN HAS FOUND A PLACE IN YOUR HEART AND THAT THERE'S A LITTLE SPACE IN THERE FOR ME TOO. I'LL BE HERE, WAITING FOR YOU WHENEVER YOU WANT TO RETURN. THIS CITY HAS PLENTY MORE TO DISCOVER!

KEEP TRAVELING AND ALWAYS LOOK AT THE WORLD WITH EYES FULL OF WONDER.

AUF WIEDERSEHEN!

LAURA RE

Born in Rome, Laura attended the Scuola Romana del Fumetto. She later collaborated with animation studios in the role of character designer, concept artist, and illustrator. After attending the International School of Illustration in Sarmede, Italy, she moved to Milan to complete the Illustration Master Class at Mimaster. There she deepened her knowledge of publishing and illustration for children.

DANIELA CELLI

Born in Florence in 1977, Daniela studied piano at the Luigi Cherubini Conservatory before moving to New York to study criminology. She returned to Italy in 1997 and graduated in law while also obtaining a diploma at the Accademia d'Arte Drammatica. A long-time travel enthusiast, she has been blogging about adventures around the world with her family since 2008.

Graphic layout: Valentina Figus

WS whitestar kids™ is a trademark of White Star s.r.l.

Piazzale Luigi Cadorna, 6
20123 Milan, Italy
www.whitestar.it

Translation: Qontent
Editing: Michele Suchomel-Casey

First printing, March 2025

ISBN 978-88-544-2140-0
1 2 3 4 5 6   29 28 27 26 25

Printed and manufactured in China
by DONG GUAN CHUANG
DA PRINTING CO., LTD.

Herr Bär Alex lives in Berlin with his family. He likes to go on adventures, though sometimes he's a bit clumsy because of his size. But the thing he likes most of all is to lie in the park and listen to music. He loves to introduce little explorers to the city!